To grandma

A lightning storm races across Big Prairie.

It starts with a bang

The black clouds built up in the north and I knew I didn't have much time. I pulled the truck right into the path of the thunderstorm, set up the tripod and camera and hoped like heck it didn't start pouring rain.

A purple light slashed across the sky and then another and another. Boom. Boom. Boom. Most thunderstorms in Glacier come from the southwest. But this one was coming from the north.

The wind blew, the clouds darkened and there I stood in the middle of this prairie next to a metal tripod, a human lightning rod.

I set the shutter speed to bulb, the aperture to 16. And pushed down the trigger.

One one-thousand, two one-thousand, three one-thousand.

The clouds bore down on me.

Lightning slashed the sky over and over again.

Oh man, this is stupid, I thought. This is way stupid. Then it started to rain.

I let off the shutter release, and jumped into the truck.

This is how most fires start in Glacier National Park.

Huge thunderstorms with little rain and lots of lightning.

It's been happening this way for eons.

This particular storm would bring too much rain and no fires.

But in July and August and September - the driest months of the year, if a thunderstorm comes and there hasn't been any rain, you can almost count on a fire starting somewhere in Glacier National Park.

Most don't amount to much.

But in 1999, lightning started the Anaconda Fire in Glacier and burned 10,000 acres.

In 2001 lightning started the Moose Fire in the Flathead National Forest near Moose Lake. It burned thousands of acres in one day, racing into Glacier's North Fork region.

The Wedge Canyon Fire started by lightning July 18, 2003 in the Flathead National Forest and it too, raced into Glacier.

All told it burned about 30,000 acres in Glacier.

Lightning started most of the fires that have burned the Park, with the notable exception of the Robert Fire.

Like it or not, it's the nature of the landscape. Droughty summers and dry thunderstorms make for wildfires. And all of those summers were droughty - 2003, for example, was a fifth year of drought in Glacier.

The trees themselves are designed to burn.

Lodgepole pine trees, for example, grow like weeds. Thousands to an acre. The North Fork of the Flathead has huge stands of lodgepole forests. Dry them out and they're matchsticks.

Imagine this, if you will. Imagine your house is on fire

Now imagine your house and your neighbor's house on fire. That might be an acre of fire.

Now imagine your block is on fire. Every home.

That might be five acres.

I'll hand you a hose and an ax. Stoke the fire with a 30 mph wind. Now put it out.

That is wildfire.

Which isn't to say they can't be put out. When they're relatively small, they can be put out. But many wildfires have lives of their own. A fire can even create its own weather.

I watched the Wedge Canyon fire consume an entire mountainside in about a half hour. I flew

over the Moose Fire when it looked
like a nuclear bomb. The Park, for
the most part, let the Anaconda Fire
burn on its own. It threatened few
structures and was wholly in the
Park's boundary.

Why would anyone in their right
mind let a fire burn?

Because this has been happening
for eons. It's a natural part of the
landscape and there is no better
place than a National Park to let
nature take its course.

Wildfire isn't good or evil. Wildfire
simply *is*. It alters landscapes on a
grand scale. The aftermath is fasci-
nating, intriguing, dynamic and yes,
even beautiful.

You just have to get on your belly
once in a while to appreciate it.

Ground fire, Belton Hills, 2003

The Moose Fire, just outside Glacier, 2001. The forests both in and outside the Park were primed to burn, dried out by years of drought.

The Moose Fire, as seen from the air, racing into Glacier National Park, 2001.

Burnouts along Lake McDonald, August, 2003.

Visitors watch the Trapper Fire approach the Loop of the Going-to-the-Sun Road.

Trapper

I'm not sure how or why they ended up in a place like Glacier National Park, but there they were, tooling around in a compact pickup truck, in bikini tops and cut-offs, giving away free cans of Red Bull.

Red Bull is an energy drink that tastes like tin.

It was a wretchedly hot day, July 23, 2003. The wind wasn't blowing much, but there was concern it would and the Trapper Fire was sulking just north of the Going-to-the-Sun Road, waiting for a breeze.

The Trapper Fire started July 16 from lightning. In many ways, it was a classic Glacier Park wild-fire. It started naturally, was burning in a remote location north of the Going-to-the Sun Road in the narrow valley of McDonald Creek, and threat-ened virtually nothing and no one.

Until July 23, that is.

I got up on the Sun Road about 2 p.m. and watched the fire for a couple of hours. It made a plume and some smoke and torched a few trees, but nothing spectacular.

Late afternoon is always the magic time for wildfires. The sun is high and hot. Inversions have lifted. The wind picks up. Humidity is low.

Slowly, but surely, the plume of smoke from the Trapper Fire began to thicken and swirl. It grew and grew until it had a wall of flame 500 feet high and the smoke looked like a million tires on fire.

A crowd of people gathered at the Loop on the Going-to-the-Sun Road to watch. The girls in their bikini tops and cut-offs gave away Red Bull.

It was a photographer's wet dream.

Huge flames.

Chicks in bikinis.

Who could ask for anything more?

The wind kicked in and the Trapper Fire grew violently large. Folks came and went snapping pic-tures and marveling at the flames as they towered above the highway.

The Red Bull girls posed in front of the fire.

All you could hear was the roar of it.

I worked three separate cameras until the flames nearly met the pavement. The heat and smoke and ashes washed over the highway and the crowd all ran for their cars all at once.

But no one was injured. Even at Granite Park Chalet, which was above us and in the path of the fire, no one was hurt.

Two Park Service maintenance employees, Chris Burke and Mike Sanger, worked feverishly to keep folks safe while setting up sprinkler systems around the chalet, which filled with smoke and was battered by 70 mph winds.

But the flames left the structure and its guests unscathed.

Wildfires can be like that. As quickly as they spread, they can also die.

Change the humidity a few points upward and they can go from infernos to smudgepots; put the sun behind a cloud and a fire will lay down fast. A half-inch of snow will knock a massive wildfire dead out.

Past fires also play a role.

The Trapper Fire ran into the old burn from the Garden Wall Fire of 1967. The resulting vegeta-tion was different.

Gone were the pines, instead there was brush and birch and other trees that simply weren't ready to burn.

The Trapper Fire would never burn with that sort of intensity again.

As I drove out of the Park that day, a huge plume of smoke was rising in the West.

It was the Robert Fire and Glacier's fire season that summer, was just starting to cook.

The shutter clicks open and you start to count. One one thousand, two one thousand, three one thousand ... sometimes you go to only 15. Sometimes you go to 180, 240.

You capture time, and it burns brilliant reds and hues of yellow into the fabric of the film.

This is wildfire at night.

Flames are waving towers of light moved by wind.

Trees die before your eyes and their spirits shake to the heavens.

Your thumb comes off the shutter release.

The fire is roaring so loud you barely hear the click.

You go home in silence.

Say goodnight to the smoky moon.

The Robert Fire, Lake McDonald, Aug. 10, 2003, pages 12-17

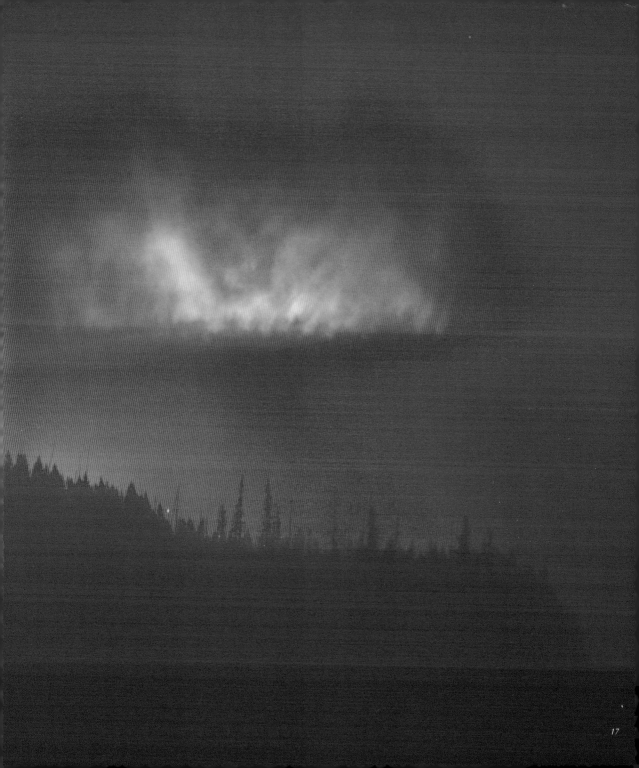

Howe Ridge burns, August, 2003.

Robert rules

I'm standing there with Columbia Falls firefighters Ron Ross and Karl Weeks and the woods in front of us are smoking, looking black.

The day is July 24, 2003. We're at a home they called North Fork One off the North Fork Road about nine miles north of Columbia Falls. From the porch, you look into Glacier National Park. We're straight in the path of the Robert Fire. Robert started the day before near an old campfire and blossomed into an inferno, racing into Glacier in just a few hours.

It was spotted by Travis Rosenkotter, a lookout at the Huckleberry Lookout in Glacier. He named the fire after his father.

Now Robert was also moving North, heading right at us.

Ross has just sprayed the home with a goop that's designed to keep it from catching on fire when the flames come.

Two other firefighters from Blankenship, Diana Waldheim and Glenn Wehe are manning a pumper.

You can hear the fire in the woods below the house. You can see smoke billowing above us as well. We're surrounded by fire. We just don't know it, because we can't *see*.

But we can hear it coming and it doesn't sound good. Robert is growling, just off the ledge, down in that river bottom.

Part of saving a house from a wildfire is to clear stuff that might catch on fire - like brush and trees and junk - away from the home. That's pretty much already been done with one exception. There are two huge propane tanks near the garage and the garage is near the woods and I'm just a little bit nervous.

Especially when Weeks tells me that one of those little tanks, the kind you use on your gas grill, can level a city block.

"When the fire hits those trees," Weeks says, pointing to the forest out the front yard, "we're out of here."

No one is arguing.

And then the flames are in the trees. The lodgepoles at first pop and crackle and seem startled by the heat and then they roar into flame, one after another.

As everyone jumps into their trucks the flames close in on the driveway. The driveway squeezes through the woods and the trees are popping into flame and just as we squeeze out into the road I remember this: The trees are on fire and a helicopter swoops over us and drops a load of water just as the trees, not feet from the engine, burst into flames.

Holycrapholycrapholycrap. It becomes a chant, running through your mind.

We make it out OK to a place down the road called the safe zone. The safe zone looks like it's been hit with a nuclear bomb. Trees are black or burning and the air is sick with smoke. As the trees burn, they fall over. Ba-boom. Ba-boom.

It is a safe zone because it has already burned, for the most part.

But you learn right quick to stay the hell away from anything that is standing.

Helicopters buzz in the air, dropping down to the river, picking up water to dump on houses and hot spots. This is war, baby.

The birds are equipped with a huge pump and holding tank and they dangle a hose that sucks water from the river. In a matter of seconds the helicopter is hauling away 500 gallons of water.

A pump station has been set up to refill the fire engines. Fire companies from across the county are helping. The North Fork doesn't have many homes. But all of them are tucked into the woods and are vulnerable.

A lot of firefighters that day put their butts on the line to save those homes. None were lost.

We refill the fire trucks with water and head back into the fire. The goop worked and the propane tanks didn't blow.

North Fork One is left unscathed, but the trees around it are all on fire and the smoke is thick, like fog. You can't see or breathe and yet the crew works through the day putting out fires near the house, assuring nothing will spread.

You learn pretty quickly that 750 gallons of water isn't much at all.

It will barely put out a stump.

Of all the fires of 2003, the Robert Fire was the most disruptive. It filled valleys with smoke. Shut down half of Glacier National Park for weeks on end and also put on spectacular displays of fire.

On Aug. 10, 2003, Robert made another big run. Burnouts had been set in front of it on Apgar Mountain in the days before and they had worked.

A burnout is where firefighters purposefully set a fire in front of an advancing fire in order to stop its forward progress.

The method works pretty well, especially if the wind doesn't blow too hard, allowing - firefighters to control the fire they just set.

It sounds strange, but it does work. An Alaskan team of federal firefighters did a fantastic job of setting and controlling burnouts on Apgar Mountain. They probably saved West Glacier from certain demise.

But then that team left and another team from the southern U.S. came in and on Aug. 10 the wind decided to blow. It blew hard and fast and two spot fires started, jumping two roads and the fire lines.

Robert made a fantastic run that night, burning its way down Howe Ridge along Lake McDonald.

Hundreds of folks watched as the flames tore down the ridge in a torrent. The Lake McDonald Lodge was evacuated. The west side of Glacier was shut down.

Despite the fire's size and vigor, not a home was lost, not a person was injured.

I feverishly worked three cameras until the wind dropped and the flames diminished. A popular saying among photographers is that it's all about light.

That night, Robert put on a light show of historic proportions.

More than a few folks were saddened by the blaze because Glacier was drastically changed.

All I could think was, "Wow. Man, that was way cool."

Burnout, Mount Stanton, 2003. This burnout was designed to save the McDonald Creek Valley.

Smoke from the 2003 fires hangs in the McDonald Creek Valley

Loneman Peak, part of the Middle Fork Complex, burns on an August evening, 2003. The Wedge Canyon Fire burns in the North Fork, opposite page.

Recent in Glacier

1988	Red Bench	27,500
1994	Starvation Creek	4,001
1994	Howling/Anaconda/Adair	8,633
1998	Kootenai	8,758
1999	Anaconda	10,812
2001	Moose	27,194
2003	Robert	39,400
2003	Wedge Canyon	30,300
2003	Rampage Complex	21,100
2003	Trapper	18,700
2003	Wolf Gun	15,250
2003	Middle Fork Complex	10,600

In acres.

Traffic streams down U.S. Highway 2 as the Middle Fork Complex burns, August, 2003.

Many other fires also touched Glacier in 2003. There were the Middle Fork and Rampage Complex fires, started by lightning strikes on Aug. 19.

They were wholly contained inside the Park boundaries along the remote southern boundary of the Park.

All told, some 310,000 acres of landscape in Northwest Montana were burned in 2003 alone.

The Wedge Canyon Fire, in the North Fork of the Flathead, was the most destructive from a human standpoint. It burned down seven cabins, 29 outbuildings and damaged another home.

Burnouts were started to attempt to stop the Wedge from going to Bowman Lake.

But then the rains came.

On Sept. 8, 2003, it rained about an inch over most the fires in Northwest Montana, including Glacier National Park.

About a week later, it both rained and snowed.

With the rains came rebirth.

And the journey continues.

A combination of snow and rain puts out most of Glacier's wildfires.

A rare smile, while watching fire, August 2003.

Boy Wonder

When they tell you your son is autistic, your first reaction is to get into your car, tightly fasten your seatbelt, and drive off the nearest bridge.

Instead I went under said bridge and cried for about an hour.

Autism is a nasty affliction. A bright, loving child slowly, but surely, crawls into its own little world before your eyes. Boy Wonder, at age 2, wouldn't talk. Wouldn't potty train. Wouldn't look at you.

He was good at screaming and he could fly down the stairs on his belly.

But he walked like a drunk. And he wanted little to do with anyone else. Thus the name - Boy Wonder.

You always wondered what he was thinking. What causes autism? I don't know.

All I know is this: At around 18 months my son became very sick with the croup. Unable to breathe, his oxygen levels plummeted and he was hospitalized. Before then, he seemed to be a bright, healthy baby. When he returned he was different. His development reversed.

He used to be able to say, "Have a good day, Daddy."

Now he said nothing.

We chalked it up to the terrible twos. So did doctors.

But things never got better. They got worse. We had him tested and the prognosis was autism.

He might get better. He might not. Intensive therapies seemed to be the most productive. So we started on our own, borrowing from a host of different treatments.

My wife, Sherry, is an educator by trade, so she started him out on intensive one-on-one speech, occupational, and physical therapy programs.

We also changed his diet. Many autistic children, it turns out, are allergic to wheat and dairy products. We took them away.

Progress was achingly slow. For my part, I decided a rather simple program. I would take him to Glacier and we would hike. I was working on this book, and he'd have to come along, like it or not.

Fortunately, Glacier was one of the few places he didn't complain about. He loved the water. And at the time, he especially liked rocks.

Day after day, hour after hour, we hiked and threw rocks into rivers and lakes and streams.

It turned into something constructive.

Instead of just allowing him to throw rocks on his own (which he was happy to do, completely ignoring me) I made him give me the rocks and then I would throw them. Or vice versa.

"To me," I'd say. He'd hand me a rock. I'd throw it.

"To you," I'd say. I'd hand him a rock. He would throw it.

Then I got to picking up big rocks and throwing them in the lake.

That would make him laugh and for an instant we would make eye contact and he would smile.

This was progress.

The hikes were painfully slow. I am a hiker that thinks nothing of going 15 to 18 miles in a day. Suddenly, I was hiking with a child who, when we first started out, could do maybe a half-mile — a mile on a good day.

He'd walk a short ways and then sit down and sift dirt through his fingers. I'd pick him up and prod him on. He'd go a few more feet and sit down and sift dirt through his fingers again.

Stimulatory behavior is common in autistic children. Getting beyond it is a major hurdle. He went from sifting dirt to insisting on dragging a stick along. The sticks got bigger and bigger until they were the size of small trees.

Then he abandoned dragging the sticks for an orange. He carried an orange around for months. Every time we went to the grocery store, we picked up a fresh one.

A friend once made the mistake of peeling it. Boy Wonder had a meltdown. He outgrew the orange. It took forever, a whole summer of hikes.

He went through obsessive phases like this that lasted months. One would stop. Another would start.

By the end of the summer of his third year he was hiking seven miles a week, a mile at a time.

That was 2001. The Moose Fire was scorching Glacier.

At the same time I had my own growing fascination with the after-effects of all these fires. Fires are life-changing events. And so is autism.

Fortunately, many of the trails and places that led into burned areas suited the affliction. They were flat, easy to get to, and extremely interesting. Perfect for an autistic boy. Perfect for his photographer father.

Therapy became work. Work became therapy. We had our own obsessions. We tolerated each other's quirks. We became best of friends.

By the summer of 2005, knocking off a four or five mile hike was the norm, rather than the exception.

He still didn't talk very well, but the child who, four years ago, would barely look at me, now communicated almost entirely through eye contact — looks and glances and wonderful, huge smiles.

He had gone from a kid who could barely walk to a monkey - climbing trees, skipping down rocky slopes with a fleetness his clumsy father could only watch and admire.

If it wasn't for him, I likely would have never hiked the places I did or seen the things I saw.

The owls. The flowers. The moose. The bears. The mushrooms. The insects. The frogs. The fish. The deer.

The list goes on and on.

The landscape accommodated us. Welcomed us. Taught us lessons. Gave us joy. Challenged us and rewarded us.

"Wow man," you think to yourself. "There is a God."

**Previous page: A last look ;
was razed by the Moose Fir**

favorite meadow in 2005. Above: Taking a break to play on a beaver dam. The swamp behind him

Arnica mass blooms after wildfire, as does fireweed, opposite.

Revival

Glacier lilies bloom en masse in the Wedge Canyon burn, spring, 2004.

Burned aspen not only provide great nesting trees, they also sprout new groves after wildfire.

Wild hollyhocks bloom in the Robert Fire, summer, 2005.

Lupine and paintbrush in the Moose burn.

Doe and fawn in elegant pine grass, summer 2005, Robert burn.

Camas in the Moose burn.

The Morel of the story

The ranger's car screeched to a halt and he got out and walked over to where I was. I was with Boy Wonder in a burned and blackened patch of lodgepole pine, photographing arnica, a flower that dots up here and there in a normal forest, but has huge mass flowerings after a fire.

The ranger recognized me.

"Oh," he said. "It's just you."

He sounded a little disappointed.

I smiled.

The rangers were out after morel mushroom pickers.

Morel mushrooms, for reasons that aren't entirely clear, can sprout up in the millions after fire.

Add a little moisture to the blackened earth and the reproductive parts of the fungus, sprout up and they go through a mass "flowering" event, if you will.

Incredibly edible, the tasty mushrooms also bring top dollar. There's a whole legion of collectors who follow the wildfires through the West, hoping to make a quick buck off the books.

In the Flathead National Forest, pickers set up camps and were allowed to gather mushrooms for a small fee. Most of the guys I met were desperately poor Vietnamese immigrants who came from the coast.

They lived in makeshift camps and drove ramshackle rigs. The camps looked like something out of the Grapes of Wrath, only they were picking mushrooms, not fruit.

While picking mushrooms in the Forest was legal, picking mushrooms in the Park is decidedly illegal.

So the rangers did their patrols and caught a few guys, most who were heavily armed because they were deathly afraid of bears.

The benefit for a guy like me, of course, was that mushrooms were easy to find and easy to photograph in Glacier.

Photographing them means getting on your belly, down low and personal.

Of course, Boy Wonder, seeing me in this state, got great delight in helping me out.

He'd come over and jump on my back and then laugh — like no tomorrow.

The favorite shot is the one on the next two pages.

It's a little village. All the mushroom on the right needs is a little door and a Hobbit, if you will, sweeping the porch.

Morel mushrooms in Robert burn, 2004.

The lesson

The post-fire cycle on one level might work something like this: The fire enriches the soil, which, in turn, encourages new plant growth. The new plant growth then feeds rodents like chipmunks or voles or mice, which in turn feed owls and hawks and yes, even the occasional hungry bear.

The rodents also bury the seeds and spread the seeds which encourages even more plant growth and more rodents which help more predatory birds and so on and so forth.

But this is just one level. One instance.

Nature, however, is series of levels upon levels.

Chains upon chains.

Reactions to reactions.

And in all of this, as I slowly put the pieces together, I'm also showing this stuff to Boy Wonder.

"What is that?" I ask, pointing at the chipmunk.

No answer.

So I tell him.

"It's a chipmunk," I say. "Say chipmunk."

"Chick-munk," he says.

"No, chipmunk," I correct him.

"Chick-munk," he says.

"Chipmunk," I say.

"Chick-munk," he says.

Sigh.

Fireweed is pervasive several years after a fire.

Not all fires
are equal

Some landscapes revive more slowly than others. Rainfall the following year plays a role, as does the severity and location of the burn.

But even in the Trapper Fire, which burned extremely hot in some places, I was surprised to find herds of healthy mule deer, feeding on the sparse but sweet new vegetation in what was largely a sea of black.

Of course, stand replacement fires like this aren't good for all species. For example, tree squirrels and pine martens don't generally survive them and in the winter, severely burned areas provide little shelter for ungulate species.

With more than 7 inches of rain in June, 2005, the post-Robert Fire environment turned lush with new vegetation. This bull moose was a frequent visitor, feeding both in and around Fish Creek, which was razed by the blaze.

A ghost in the trees

November, 2004, this white-tailed buck was pursuing does in the Robert Fire burn near Fish Creek. Both mule deer and whitetails called the burn home.

McGee Meadow, razed by Robert, lush by June, 2005.

Purple aster, Robert burn, summer, 2004.

Bears

A grizzly bear prowls the Moose burn, 2004. Photo was taken from the safety of a car.

One of our favorite hikes went through the trees and then opened up into a meadow, through a burn and then to a swamp where the beavers lived.

We would stop and take pictures along the way and Boy Wonder would chase frogs and climb in trees and play on the beaver dam.

Sometimes we would fish.

Sometimes we would just sit around and watch the world go by.

It is a beautiful valley by any standard - a big chunk of it was burned by the Moose fire in 2001.

Another chunk by the Robert Fire in 2003.

In the middle there were live trees and swamps and in some places, the landscape went slowly from being burned to dense old-growth forest.

The valley was also what folks would call a bear's nest. You didn't just happen upon bear tracks here. You expected them. Big bears. Little bears.

They walked the trail just like you and I would walk the trail.

The nice thing about hiking with Boy Wonder is that he always made a noise of some sort. Mostly he would gab away about some video he'd seen. Other days he'd just groan a little. He was never quiet.

They say you should yell and shout in bear country to let bears know you are coming and that is true, you should. But as a photographer, you also have to see with your ears and you'll often hear something long before you ever see it.

So if you're yelling "hey bear," all the time, you see little because you can't hear while you're yelling.

It's just one of those things.

But if you have a kid along making noise you can still hear other stuff.

It was a relationship that worked out well. He made the noise. I kept watch.

He'd chase frogs. I'd watch birds. He'd climb trees. I'd photograph flowers.

All the while, I'm pretty sure the bears knew we were there. One thing was for sure, the bears didn't leave because of the fires. If anything, they seemed to thrive. This particular drainage has the highest concentration of bears in Glacier, a recent study of grizzly bears in the Park has shown.

That didn't surprise me.

Bears seemed to have adapted to the fires quite nicely. What food supplies were lost initially seemed to be regained in other areas.

For example, some folks predicted it would take decades for berry bushes to grow back. Not true. Serviceberries abounded in the burns, just a couple of years after the fires.

Glacier lilies sprouted up in places they hadn't been before. The root of the glacier lily is bear candy. White, bright and sweet, like a carrot.

Bears also pigged out on ants in dead trees. It was nothing to see a dead tree flopped over and torn up by a hungry griz.

But like I said, while we saw bear sign everywhere nearly every day, we rarely saw a bear.

Bears are a crepuscular creature, most active at dawn and dusk. We hiked that area probably 25 times in the summer of 2005. We fell into a rhythm, a routine. For Boy Wonder, it was a great place to play. For me, it was a great place to work.

Then on one hard, hot sunny afternoon, we got a friendly reminder of whose home this really was.

We were walking through a burn and I looked up and there was a big, black grizzly.

It moved through the fireweed and downed trees, a wave of bristling black fur.

"Hey, bear, hey bear!" I yelled.

The bear never looked up. Never stopped. It came directly in our direction, then slightly off to the left and then disappeared into the woods.

"Damn," I whispered. "That was one big bear."

A grizzly in the moose burn (previou

page). Shaking off after rolling in the wet grass.

A black bear cub and sow feed on new grass in the Robert burn, spring, 2004. Bears graze on grass and new vegetation when they first awake from hibernation.

The Who

"'mon," I said to Boy Wonder. "Let's go over to the other side of this meadow. You can climb that big tree."

One of the really cool things that happens after fire are the flowers. Dump a little rain on this scorched Earth and seeds that have been literally waiting for decades, sprout, grow and bloom.

Paintbrush. Hollyhocks. Fireweed. Geraniums. Asters. Glacier lilies. Arnica. And on and on.

It all starts when the snow melts the spring after a fire. In this meadow, on this day, it was blankets of shooting stars, a small purple flower. You usually see one here and there. Not a whole field of them.

June 2005 was particularly wet. The Park saw 7.5 inches of rain in West Glacier and the place just exploded with flowers. It was as if the plant world had been waiting for the exact time, the exact moment, to go forth and multiply.

So we walked along the edge of the meadow to the big dead tree that was down, a blackened beast that had lost its roots to fire and toppled over.

Boy Wonder immediately took to it, climbing to the upper edge of its exposed root system, which stuck a good eight feet out of the ground.

And that's when I heard it. A distinctive cry. A croaky wail coming from the other side of the brush and downed trees. There was a stand of aspen, some burned and dead, others still very much alive between us and the sound.

Aspens are a particularly wonderful tree in a post-fire world. When fire gets in them it hollows out a host of nooks and crannies in the heart of the wood, making perfect homes for a host of birds and other small mammals. In many cases, not every tree is killed in the fire, either. The live trees, in turn, offer cover and shade to the critters living in the dead trees.

Additionally, aspens shoot up new trees in groves as a result of fires. These saplings can

Northern Hawk Owl fledglings in the Moose Fire

n, above and previous page, spring, 2005.

grow at a rate of several feet a year. What you end up with is a successional forest, a dynamic landscape of death, life and rebirth.

And coming out of it was this strange sound. This plaintive wail. Boy Wonder and I went in to investigate.

Now following the cries of something in distress is not always a smart move in Glacier, for it could be something far bigger than you, like a grizzly bear, eating something. There are two things grizzly bears don't enjoy very much. One is having their cubs even remotely threatened. The other is having their meals disturbed. They have a tendency to attack and kill you in those situations.

So I plowed ahead, hoping like hell it wasn't a bear on the other side of the bushes.

As we went I saw a warbler and I thought, "That is a very strange call from such a pretty yellow bird."

And then a raven called and I heard the clack of talons against feathers and I looked up to see a smallish owl after the raven, driving it away, high in the treetops.

The calls continued. Boy Wonder and I made it through the brush and there they were. The warbler was not making this strange sound. Three strange little owls were making this strange sound. Squawking and crying and carrying on. The raven had heard them and saw an easy lunch. The parents of these fledglings, had different ideas.

I unloaded the camera gear from my pack and captured them all on film. The fledglings couldn't quite fly, but had fallen from the nest. They had long bodies and long tails and while they were unmistakably owls, they sure didn't act like them. They seemed vulnerable until one scanned the treetops. The parents perched high in the trees and kept watch over them.

Help was just a swoop away.

The evening turned to dusk and Boy Wonder and I left, curious as to what this strange bird may be.

The call of a Northern Hawk owl fledgling is unn

...akably distinctive.

My purpose for this journey was to remain completely open to discovery. I would photograph things first, Find out what they were second. I was sort of a virgin who was deflowered by science on a regular basis.

My owls (I called them that, once to a bird watcher who came up behind me out of the blue. She startled me and I blurted out, like an idiot, "I found them first.") were northern hawk owls. Northern Hawk owls are found in Canada and Alaska, but in Glacier they had been exceedingly rare sights.

But in the spring of 2005, with all that rain and all that food suddenly available, the vole population took off and the owls for whatever reason, not only found the Park, but made it their home.

Within about a three kilometer circle, four nesting pairs of hawk owls were found.

The owls I stumbled upon that day in May were the fourth pair.

Through the coming weeks, Boy Wonder and I would watch them grow up. They learned to fly quickly. The mature owls are masters of flight. They're also terrorists. They hunt both night and day and their call is very un-owl like. It's more of a trill, a pleasant whistle.

Sure, the fledglings still squawked and the parents squawked back, but when the adults were alone, their call took on a quality like no other I've ever heard, as nice as a warbler, maybe more so.

The pleasant call aside, living with hawk owls was difficult if you were another small bird or mammal. I watched one eat a junco whole, and found a fledgling on another day eating a ravaged snipe its parents had killed for it.

Voles weren't the only critter on the menu, though I did see them get snared as well.

The northern hawk owls weren't the only ones taking advantage of this new landscape, either. A pair of great gray owls also frequented the area and raised young as well.

The great gray is the tallest of owls. The Moose

Great gray owl fledgling on a burned snag.

Fire, in this particular drainage, had burned up one side of a creek and deep into the valley. But on the other side of the creek the woods remained fairly intact. This provided a unique habitat of open spaces of meadows and burned forests and thick, deep, mature woods.

A virtual owl paradise. We ran into the great gray and two fledglings in our travels on several occasions.

One evening, while returning from a hike, the great gray was perched in a tree just ahead of us.

Boy Wonder and I stopped.

The big hurdle in raising autistic kids is getting them to talk. With Boy Wonder, he could take things in. I mean, he understands words and phrases, but he always has had a tough time getting words out.

The great gray dropped off its perch and flew not five feet from his head, landing in a tree just a few yards away.

"What was that?" I asked him.

"It was an owl," he said, plain as day.

A great gray owl hunts from a burned snag.

For an owl, the great gray is a tall bird.

A northern hawk owl adult with a junco. Hawk owls
hunt both night and day, and have a very pleasant trill.

Great gray fledgling. The owls made a burned-over aspen stand home.

A three-toed woodpecker in the Robert burn.

Knock, knock

You don't want to tell anybody you've been out looking for wood-peckers.

It's the sort of thing you don't brag about.

"What did you do this weekend?"

"I was out looking for woodpeckers."

"You did what?"

"Nothing. I didn't do anything this weekend. Honest."

Woodpeckers don't have the charm of owls or eagles or hawks. They're woodpeckers for crying out loud.

But in the fall of 2004, almost exactly a year after the Robert Fire scorched a black path through Glacier, the place was woodpeckerville.

Boy Wonder and I, of course, found them entirely by accident. It's not like we went out looking for them. Honest. Swear on the Holy Bible.

One of our favorite hikes that year was to Howe Lake. It was a nice little two-mile hike in and out, right through the heart of the Robert Fire.

It was perfect for a 7-year-old. Boy Wonder was over his orange car-rying phase and pretty much over dragging sticks. Sure, he still groaned and carried on, but he was getting noticeably better.

The obsession turned to climbing trees. He especially enjoyed trees that were leaning over but not completely down.

So I'd look for woodpeckers. Boy Wonder would climb trees and groan and recite lines from his favorite cartoons.

"Cub! Cub! Where are you?" he'd say — a line from the Little Bear movie.

Or another favorite from Little Bear: Little Bear and his old man are walking through the woods on a fishing trip and Little Bear goes and climbs a waterfall and his old man tells him to be careful and the dia-logue goes like this:

"Be careful. What? I said, 'Be careful,' I know, it's beautiful."

And so on and so forth — Boy Wonder in the trees, reciting lines or groaning.

The woodpeckers didn't care. And there were woodpeckers out the wazoo in those burned forests.

In one day in one hour I counted no less than four different species. Black-backed woodpeckers, three-toed woodpeckers, pileated woodpeckers and downy woodpeckers.

According to biologists much smarter than I, there are beetle species that detect smoke and heat. They begin to infest forests almost as soon as the fire passes through.

Their larvae then bore into the trees and feed on the wood.

The woodpeckers then go after the larvae. I found it particularly true in forests of large larch that were killed by fire.

Seeing woodpeckers and photographing them, however, are two different things. Fall in Glacier can bring glorious days. But more often than not, it brings clouds and rain.

So Boy Wonder and I went back and back and back again.

I ended up with a handful of usable images.

On the walks home, we played monster. I was the monster. He was the poor little kid, running away.

The drooling monster would chase the poor little kid, all the way back to the truck.

You never saw a kid laugh so hard.

A black-backed woodpecker in the Robert burn.

A short tale about Toads

In the summers after the burns, scientists from the United States Geological Survey fitted some boreal toads with radio collars. Well, not collars per se, but belts that fit around their waist. What they found was that toads seemed like to burns the summers immediately after the fires. They bred there. They ate there. They slept there.

Once the area starts to grow back, the toads, over the course of years, use the area less and less.

Why, exactly, this happens, scientists aren't quite sure.

But they suspect that Glacier's amphibians, in general, benefit from wildfire cycles.

The Forest

It is April, 2006, and Boy Wonder and I are walking through a burn, although looking at it, you would never know.

Lodgepole pine 100 feet tall tower above us and the only remnants of any sort of fire whatsoever are stumps, graying and thick with moss.

The Fire of 1929 burned through here. It used to be cedar and hemlock forests, but those were razed by the fire.

But if you look closely, if you pay attention, you will see that here and there, there are hemlocks and there are cedars. In fact there are a lot of cedars and hemlocks.

Boy Wonder's gait is easy and free and joyous. He has no problem keeping up.

On this day you see ducks and geese and three swans in the creek.

You stop and take a break at a big old stump.

Growing out of the old hemlock stump is a hemlock seedling, just a foot high.

The night before you picked up a pen and a piece of paper and wrote a simple word down. That word was Hop.

You showed it to Boy Wonder and he looked at it and said, sounding it out,

"H ... huh."

"O ... uh."

"P ... puh."

"Hop," he said, reading the word, all by himself.

This comes from a boy that just a few years ago wouldn't look at you, could barely walk.

And as you walk through this forest with your son you glance back and notice that he is following your footsteps exactly.

And now you know what they were talking about, when they said you have to see the forest through the trees.

There are many people who made this book possible and
they all deserve a special thanks: Becky Shay, who proofread
the first drafts; Suzanne and Richard Garlough, who watched
Boy Wonder when I was chasing fires; to his sisters, for their
patience; Steve Gniadek and Dennis Divoky of Glacier
National Park; Steve Corn of the USGS, and of course,
my wife, Sherry.

First edition

A Glacier Geographic Book

www.glaciergeographic.com

*A note about the bear photos in this book. They were all
taken from the safety of a vehicle. Never approach or
feed a bear. Also, the wildlife photos were taken with long
telephoto lenses to minimize disturbance. Please respect all of
Glacier's wild creatures.*

ISBN # 0-9785354-0-5

Printed in HongKong